The Shelly's Adventures Series

Shelly Goes to New York

Kentrell Martin

To the Reader

Throughout the book, Shelly's hands demonstrate how
each highlighted word is signed in American Sign Language (ASL).
You will find an alphabet chart at the end of the book.

Shelly Goes to New York by Kentrell Martin
Also in The Shelly's Adventures Series: *Shelly Goes to a Fiesta* (English and Spanish), *Shelly Goes to the Zoo, Shelly's Outdoor Adventure, Shelly Meets a New Friend, Shelly Goes to the Bank, Kasey's First Day of Basketball Practice* and *KJ's Emotional Day.*

ISBN: 978-1-953768-02-5
Library of Congress Control Number: 2020921778

Published by Shelly's Adventures LLC
Website: www.shellysadventuresllc.com

Printed and bound in the USA

Illustrations by ePublishing eXperts
Book design by Jill Ronsley, Sun Editing & Book Design, suneditwrite.com

Shelly's Adventures LLC was created to provide children and their parents with reading material that teaches American Sign Language. Shelly's Adventures LLC produces materials that make signing fun for kids, parents and teachers.

Kentrell Martin believes that New York City
is one of the most fascinating cities in the world.
This book was written to give young readers
a glimpse of what it has to offer.

"Today we are going to one of my favorite places," says Shelly.
"Where?" Maria asks.
"California?" Kasey guesses.
"No," says Shelly. "We are going to New York. New York City, to be exact." She signs NEW YORK.

"New York"
Slide "Y" hand forward and back over the other hand.

"I heard that New York City is one of the largest cities in the world," says Amber. "It is," says Shelly, "and it's the largest city in the United States."

"Wow! How many people live here?" says Maria.
"More than eight million people live in
New York City," Shelly replies.
Shelly shows them the sign for PEOPLE.

"People"
Move both "P" fingers in a circle.

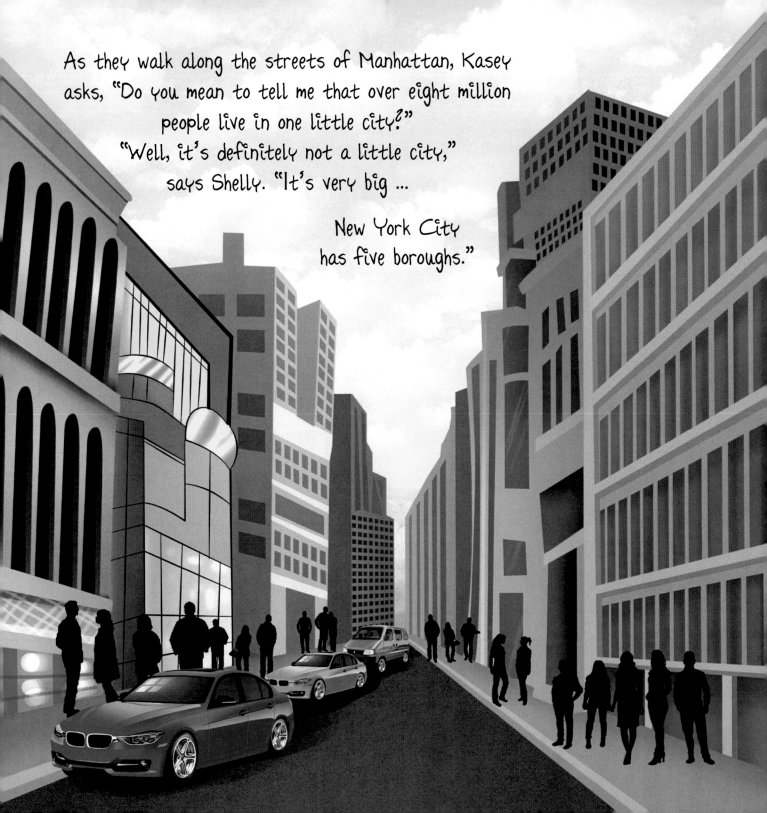

As they walk along the streets of Manhattan, Kasey asks, "Do you mean to tell me that over eight million people live in one little city?"

"Well, it's definitely not a little city," says Shelly. "It's very big ...

New York City has five boroughs."

THE 5 BOROUGHS OF NEW YORK CITY

"The five boroughs of New York City are Manhattan, Brooklyn, Queens, Staten Island and the Bronx," Shelly explains. "We're in Manhattan now, but we're going to stop in all of the boroughs before we leave."

THE BRONX

MANHATTAN

QUEENS

BROOKLYN

STATEN ISLAND

"Where is Harlem?" Kasey asks. "I thought it was in New York City too."

Shelly replies, "Harlem is part of Manhattan. Maybe we can stop there before we leave."

After lunch, Amber asks," How do all these people get around the city?"
"Some people walk, and some catch the bus, a taxi or the train," says Shelly.
"I've never been on a train before," says Maria. "Can we catch the train?"
"Sure. Let's take a train," says Shelly.

She shows them
the sign for TRAIN.

"Train"
Slide top 2 fingers
back and forth.

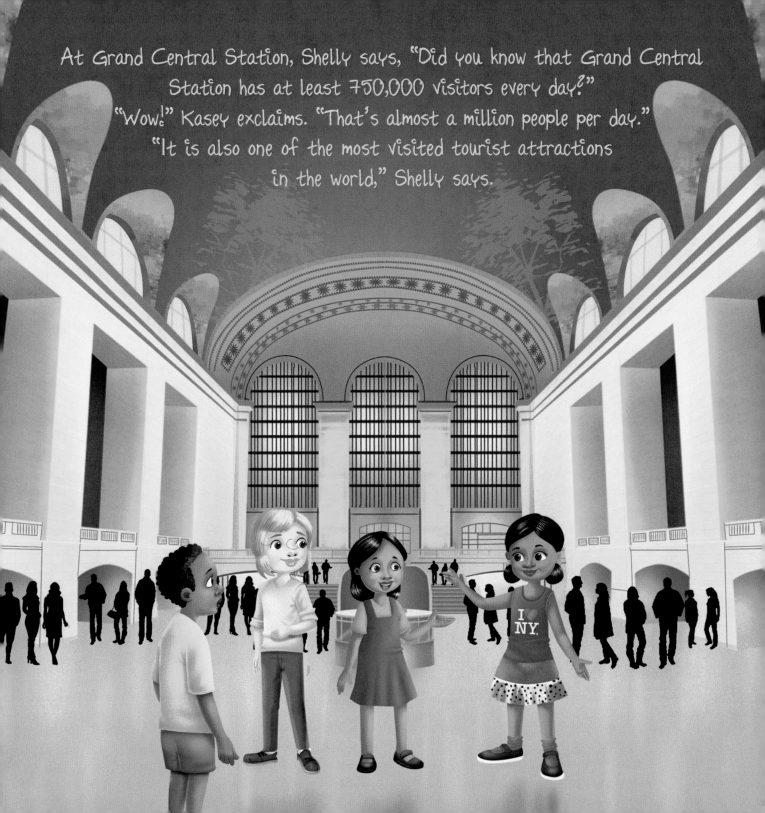

At Grand Central Station, Shelly says, "Did you know that Grand Central Station has at least 750,000 visitors every day?"

"Wow!" Kasey exclaims. "That's almost a million people per day."

"It is also one of the most visited tourist attractions in the world," Shelly says.

After riding a train to Brooklyn, Maria says,
"This is the busiest place I've ever visited."
"New York City is one of the busiest places
in the world," says Shelly.

She shows them the
sign for BUSY.

"Busy"
Move B hand left and right.

In Brooklyn Bridge Park,
they see a bridge.

Amber shouts, "Look at that bridge!
That's the biggest bridge I've ever seen."
Kasey says, "I wonder how long it took them to build it."

Shelly says, "That is the Brooklyn Bridge. It's one of the iconic bridges in the world. It goes from here to Manhattan, and it took fourteen years to build. It's more than 125 years old, and over 150,00 vehicles cross it every day."

Shelly shows them the sign for BRiDGE before they continue their walk.

"Bridge"

Move 2 fingers from the wrist towards the elbow.

Kasey asks, "Where is the famous statue of the lady with her hand raised?"
Maria says, "Are you talking about the Statue of Liberty?"
Kasey replies, "Yes, the one that looks like this!"

He poses like
the Statue of Liberty.
They all laugh.

Shelly says, "The Statue of Liberty is in the New York Harbor. We can see it if we catch the ferry to Staten Island."

Amber says, "I've always wanted to see the Statue of Liberty."

Maria is so excited on the ferry.
"There it is!" she shouts.
Kasey says, "Wow! That's a big statue!"
Maria asks," How tall is it, Shelly?"
Shelly replies, "The Statue of Liberty is 305 feet tall, and it weighs 450,000 pounds."

After exploring Staten Island, Amber says, "We've seen so much today." Maria agrees, saying, "I know. What's next?"

"My feet are starting to hurt," says Kasey. "How much do New Yorkers walk? I feel like I've walked around the world and back."
They all laugh.
Shelly says, "We have two more boroughs to visit—Queens and the Bronx. Then we can head back to Manhattan to see the bright lights."

In Queens, Maria says. "I see a lot of sports fans on the street. Does a sports team play here?" Shelly replies, "New York City has at least eight professional sports teams."

Kasey perks up and says, "My favorite New York teams are the Yankees and the Brooklyn Nets. I used to like the New York Knicks, but I don't anymore."

"Traitor!" Amber jokes.

YANKEE STADIUM

They debate over their favorite New York teams
for a few minutes before heading to the Bronx.
In the Bronx, they visit Yankee Stadium and the Bronx Zoo."

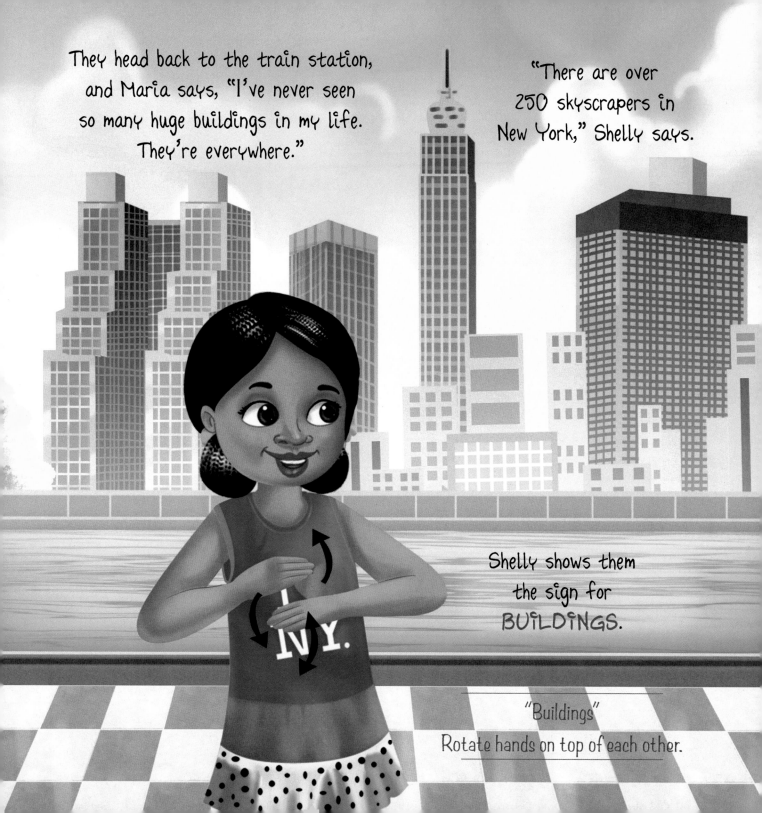

They head back to the train station, and Maria says, "I've never seen so many huge buildings in my life. They're everywhere."

"There are over 250 skyscrapers in New York," Shelly says.

Shelly shows them the sign for BUILDINGS.

"Buildings"
Rotate hands on top of each other.

Back on the train, Kasey asks, "Are there other parks in
New York City like the park in Brooklyn?"
Shelly replies, "Yes, New York City has many big parks.
Some of the most popular ones are Central Park, Prospect Park,
Washington Square Park, Brooklyn Bridge Park and Bryant Park."

"That's a lot of
parks!" says Maria.

When they arrive back in Manhattan,
Amber asks, "Is there a famous street here?"
Maria asks, "The street that the
Macy's Thanksgiving Parade goes on?"
Shelly says, "Yes, it goes down 77th Street.
There are many popular streets in New York."

BROADWAY

5 AV

"Some that you might have heard of are Wall Street, 5th Avenue, Broadway, Madison Avenue, Park Place and Lexington Avenue. We hear these street names often, but there are more."

Shelly shows them the sign for STREET.

"Street"
Move both hands forward.

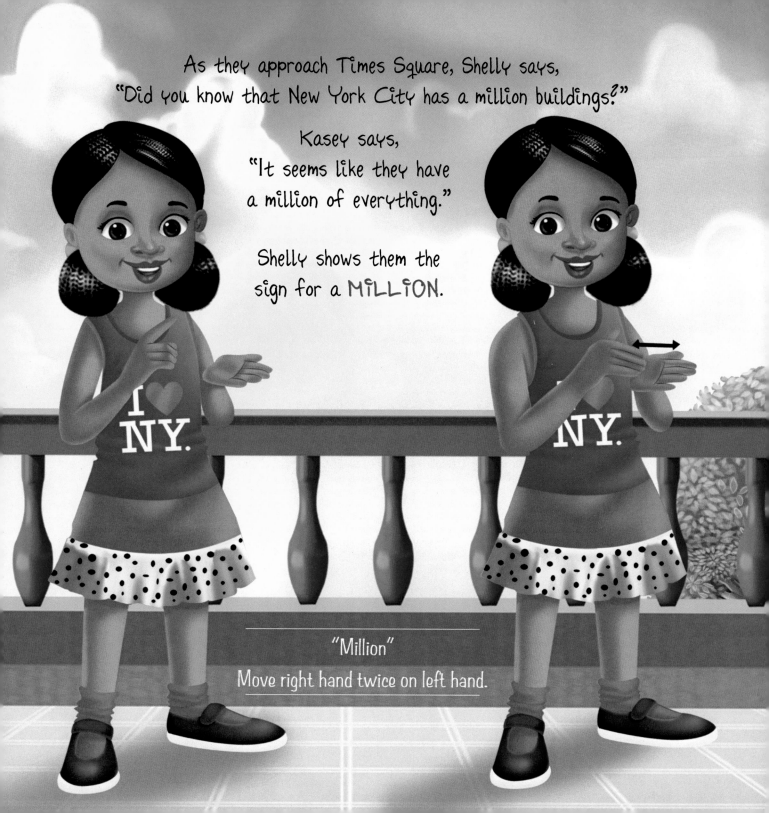

As they approach Times Square, Shelly says,
"Did you know that New York City has a million buildings?"

Kasey says,
"It seems like they have
a million of everything."

Shelly shows them the
sign for a MILLION.

"Million"
Move right hand twice on left hand.

As the sun sets, the buildings light up.
Kasey says, "I love these bright lights!"
Maria says, "I do too."

"Are we in Times Square?" Amber asks.
Shelly says, "Yes, Times Square is a famous place
in New York that is visited by many tourists."

"This is so cool" Amber says.
"I can see why New York is called the
city that never sleeps," says Kasey. "It's
not possible when it's always so bright."
Shelly laughs and shows them the sign
for BRIGHT.

"Bright"
Move both hands to
the open position.

After enjoying the bright city lights for a while, Kasey asks, "Can we please go to Harlem before we go home? I want to visit and learn more about its history." "Yes," Shelly says. "Tomorrow we can spend the day there and learn all about it."

Shelly signs TOMORROW, and they walk back to their hotel on 5th Avenue.

"Tomorrow"
Rotate thumb towards
the front of face.

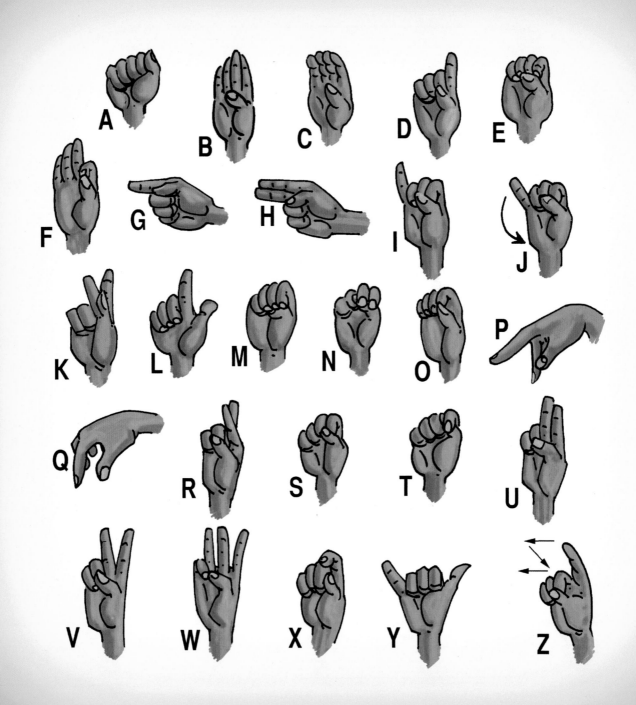

THE SHELLY's ADVENTURES SERIES

CHAPTER BOOKS

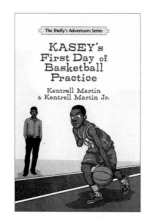

PICTURE BOOKS

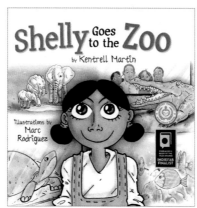

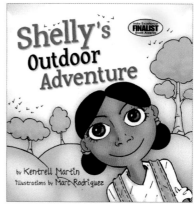

More exciting titles by
Kentrell Martin
coming soon!

Visit Us

Visit our website www.shellysadventures.com to learn
more about Shelly's Adventures and to
sign up for our mailing list and get the latest deals.

Visit www.shellysadventuresacademy.com to learn
more about the Shelly's Adventures ASL Academy.

Visit author Kentrell Martin's Youtube at
https://www.youtube.com/user/ShellysAdventuresLLC.

If you'd like to invite Kentrell to your next event
please send an email to booking@shellysadventures.com.

If you have a moment, please leave us a review on
Amazon to let us know how you liked the book.

Made in the USA
Columbia, SC
07 March 2023

13020390R00020